HER THOUGHTS

S.A.Malik

AURAQ

Printed in the Islamic Republic of Pakistan.
Printed: October, 2020
Edition: 1st
ISBN: 978-969-749-033-2
Price: Rs 850 PKR, $08 US

ISLAMABAD, PAKISTAN

raabta@auraqpublications.com.pk | +92-300-0571-530
www.auraqpublications.com.pk | @AuraqPublications
ISBN : 978-969-749-033-2

For all those who believed

In me when I couldn't believe in

Myself

Contents

Poetry

'She is a woman'

She is strong and fierce, yet fragile and delicate

She has a storm inside her, yet she can calm your nerves,

She expects too much, but she is only willing to do it such,

She can be inherently emotional and empathetic, but that's her superpower

She loves passionately, but she knows no other way,

She is independent, but sometimes she needs a shoulder to cry on,

She is all these facets and more,

She is a woman!

S.A Malik

'Let's Give Peace A Chance'

Peace and love are intertwined, in the infinite cycle of life,

One ceases to exist without the other,

Let it bloom in our generations further,

Let's say no to arms, to guns, to war

Light a candle of hope and let peace soar,

Rise above our differences of creed, religion, race and cultures,

Tolerance should rule us supreme and refrain us from turning into vultures,

Shed the facades that separate us from one another,

Let's join our hands in the struggle for our unity,

As a family, as a brotherhood, as humanity

'My Land'

To Pakistan, my identity, my land,

I've seen you in more than 15cities,

In your numerous towns and in the grit and
determination of your people,

I've seen you in your glistening golden fields,
the pacifying blue skies,

I've smelled your sweet scent of wet mud
following the monsoon rains,

I've seen you in towering mountains of the
north paralleled by the hot and humid beaches
of the south

I've seen you in the snowy days of Quetta,

In the warmth and hospitality of Lahore,

In the beauty, calm and serenity of Islamabad,

In the hustle and bustle of Karachi,

Heard you in royal tales of Nawabs of Bahawalpur,

I have seen you in your numerous festive celebrations, in the myriad of colours

But on the other hand I have also seen you in the depths of despair, in the midst of chaos and mayhem...

Every time you surprise me with your resilience, your charisma, your charm

No matter how much circumstances try to wither you down, you come back stronger,

You have been wounded, battered and shaken but you refuse to give up,

Keep being the survivor that you are Pakistan, today and forever!

'Abuse Survivor'

She was silenced,

But her cries grew louder,

She was tortured,

But her spirit grew stronger

Every menacing look, every physical blow,

Is not a way to make her slow,

She will rise from the ashes,

She will fight her fears,

Don't think she is weak,

She is proud of her tears!

'My Saviour'

Penetrating my world like a glistening beacon of hope,

Immersing yourself in my dreams, aspirations and goals.

From a stranger, a wayfarer to a person that I call my own,

Shrouding my life with a cloak of tranquility, love and care

Diminishing my angst, melancholy and fear,

Standing tall as my biggest pillar of support and strength,

Motivating me to carve my niche and let go off pretence.

Thank you to my one and only saviour,

Who came into my life adding meaning, colour and fervour

'Disease'

I look out of the window, I hear the birds chirping,

How beautiful is everything around me,

but I feel my nerves gripping,

Day in, day out is a struggle for survival as my body shows signs of diminishing,

If only, someone could save me from this feeling of finishing,

My hands look blue, my knees keep trembling,

Hollow sunken eyes, pale skin,

My soul is free, my spirit runs wild,

I have realised I have to be my own hero,

I will no longer hide!

'Spirituality'

I will search for You,

To the depths of the prodigious oceans,

To the heights of the towering mountains,

To the limits of the expansive skies,

To here and beyond….

'Wonders of Nature'

The lake glistens like diamonds sprinkled across,

Shores embrace the valleys,

Hues of blue akin to being splattered on a canvas,

Greenery providing serenity to the eyes,

Sound of water resonates in tandem,

If there is paradise on earth, it is here!

'What is Love?'

Love is soaking in the rain while putting aside your umbrella...

With you, I am soaked to every crevice of my bones,

Drenched in the euphoria of our amalgamation...

I drink from this fountain and it quenches my thirst

Why should I look for another source?

Reflections
&
Prose

Don't let people's opinions

Drown your inner voice

Trust it,

Feed it,

Believe it!

-Self Belief-

Pain is where

the growth

starts

Stop missing

the one

who forgot

about you

Don't feel lonely,

we all come,

from the

same source

-infinity-

When someone you love

leaves,

you don't really learn to live without them,

there is a void,

which is filled with their

memories

Be true
to yourself
before you
are true
to anyone else

You can only find the

light of morning

by going through

the darkness of night

Don't try to put my spirit in shackles,

I was born to be free

Everything you are going through is preparing you for the fulfillment of your destiny,

Keep calm and enjoy the journey.

The sound of nature is

the language of God

In a world of

uncertainties,

all we look for is our own absolute

The happiness that you
are searching for everywhere,
can be found within

Life is not about reaching a destination,

but enjoying the process of your journey

All we are looking for is

a love that ignites our mind and soul

Whenever you feel that

God is denying you of something,

Believe in His Decree,

He is indeed directing you to something better

Pause. Take a Minute. Breathe.

The weight of people's judgments, lift it off your shoulders.

Remember that if God put you on this earth, there is a purpose behind it.

You were meant to be here and make the most of this precious gift of life. Don't give up on yourself!

-Mental Health-

Women should reject the age old notion of being in competition with one another , rather we should support, empower and motivate each other.

Now, we need it more than ever to be united as a gender and most importantly respect each other's opinions and differences.

-Women Empowerment -

I hope we realize that religion doesn't comprise of only praying and fasting. The most important aspect of religion is to make sure that people around you don't get hurt from your actions.

That is the essence of every religion.

-Religion-

Feminism is the most misunderstood concept.

 It is about equality of genders, not about females being superior to males.

 It is about a sense of security, about feeling safe on the roads and public places, not fearing harassment at work place, having equal opportunities for employment, having an access to education, having the freedom to express our ideas, beliefs and needs without the fear of the ramifications.

-Feminism-

Love is enabling the one

You love

Become

the best version of themselves.

Patience in the face of oppression

is not bravery.

I find peace in the sounds of nature,

Be it the sound of waves galloping in the ocean, the sound of wind swooshing against the leaves, the sound of rain pouring on the fresh mud...

For me, these sounds are the way in which God communicates with mankind, assuring us of Its Presence

If you keep believing,

You will keep receiving

Mankind has to work against the normalization of hatred, recognise that the diversity in our society enriches us and it's not a threat.

Jingoism and bigotry are used by people with vested interests to further their own agenda.

The antidote for that is simply spreading love and peace, also to accept and celebrate our differences by being more tolerant.

-Diversity and Tolerance-

When sorrows seep into your soul and

problems bow you down,

Keep trusting in God's divine plan for you,

He makes no mistakes

-Divinity-

I hear you whisper my name,

While I drift off to a land of dreams,

Where we don't need a physical touch

To be together...

-Dreams-

I don't need to look for you outside,

You reside within me,

Inside a corner of my heart,

Nestled in the memories of my brain...

Words

They can damage

And

They can heal

Choose them carefully

About the Author

Sheeba Asad studied International Human Rights at London School of Economics in UK. She is from Pakistan and has won an international award for her writing about peace from Hague University of Applied Sciences in the Netherlands. She was awarded a gold medal for her writing by Government of Pakistan. She has worked for Sindh Human Rights Commission and UNICEF where she worked on women rights and child rights. She is an advocate for women empowerment, peace and her poems have a central theme of universality and harmonious coexistence.